THE UNICORN GRATITUDE JOURNAL FOR GIRLS

The 3 Minute, 90 Day Gratitude & Mindfulness Journal

Name _ _ _ _ _ _ _ _ _ _ _ _

Starting Date

Day   Month   Year

The Life Graduate Publishing Group

Stronger Friendships

Kindness and Appreciation

The benefits of
GRATITUDE

Better Health

Increased Energy

Greater Sleep Quality

"Whatever you can do, or dream you can do, begin it .
Boldness has genius, power and magic in it."

- Johann Wolfgang von Goethe
(1749-1832)

The Importance of Gratitude

Congratulations on starting your very own Gratitude Journal. By completing your journal each day, it will help you to appreciate all of the wonderful things around you!

This journal has been created in a clear, fun and interactive one page format to make it nice and easy for you to write down how you feel, the things you enjoyed during the day and also includes spaces for drawings and to include photos if you choose.

The journal asks you to write down 2 or 3 things each day that you're grateful for. These may be things that have happened during the day, during the week or something happening in your life right now? To help you, it could be things that you do with family and friends like vacations, the accomplishments you have earned for school, sports events or activities, new friendships you have formed or anything else that you are grateful for.

Just sparing 3 minutes each day to think about the things in life that matter to you will boost your confidence and energy levels and you will take new leaps and bounds every day.

Gratitude and mindfulness activities like journaling are so important, and we all need to think about what we are grateful for every day.

Wishing you all the very best!

Romney

Romney Nelson - Teacher & Multiple Best Selling Author
Founder - The Life Graduate Publishing Group
www.thelifegraduate.com

MY UNICORN GRATITUDE JOURNAL

DATE: MON TUES WED THU FRI SAT SUN ___/___/___

01 I helped this person today..

Write below what you did to be kind.....

02 Gratitude. These are 3 things I am thankful for...

1 _____

2 _____

3 _____

03 I would rate today....
Color in your 'STAR' rating for today.
1 star = I didn't have a good day
5 stars = EXCELLENT!

MY UNICORN GRATITUDE JOURNAL

DATE: MON TUES WED THU FRI SAT SUN ___ / ___ / ___

01 Today I felt.....
Tick the face below...

02 Gratitude.
These are 3 things I am thankful for...

1 _____

2 _____

3 _____

03 Complete this sentence
What did you enjoy most about today?.......

Draw or Write Here

04 Today was:

MY UNICORN GRATITUDE JOURNAL

DATE: MON TUES WED THU FRI SAT SUN ___/___/___

01 My Happiness Rating

Circle how you feel?

- Happy
- Just OK
- I feel a little sad today

02 I would like to say thank you for...

1 _____
2 _____
3 _____

03 This person was kind today.

04 What did you enjoy most about today?.......

DATE: MON TUES WED THU FRI SAT SUN ___/___/___

01 Today I felt...

Draw your face here. Were you happy, laughing, nervous perhaps?

02 I felt happiest today when...

_____

03 Gratitude
These are 2 things that really make me happy!

1 _____

2 _____

04 My happiness scale today

Where did you feel on the 'Happiness' scale today?

0 = Not very good   5= OK   10 = SENSATIONAL!

MY UNICORN GRATITUDE JOURNAL

DATE: MON TUES WED THU FRI SAT SUN ___ / ___ / ___

01   I helped this person today..

Write below what you did to be kind.....

02   Gratitude. These are 3 things I am thankful for...

1 _____

2 _____

3 _____

03   I would rate today....
Color in your 'STAR' rating for today.
1 star = I didn't have a good day
5 stars = EXCELLENT!

DATE: MON TUES WED THU FRI SAT SUN ___ / ___ / ___

01 Today I felt.....
Tick the face below...

02 Gratitude.
These are 3 things I am thankful for...

1 _____

2 _____

3 _____

03 Complete this sentence
What did you enjoy most about today?.......

Draw or write here

04 Today was:

MY UNICORN GRATITUDE JOURNAL

DATE: MON TUES WED THU FRI SAT SUN ___/___/___

01 My Happiness Rating

Circle how you feel?

- Happy
- Just OK
- I feel a little sad today

02 I would like to say thank you for...

1 _____
2 _____
3 _____

03 This person was kind today.

04 What did you enjoy most about today?.......

DATE: MON TUES WED THU FRI SAT SUN ___ / ___ / ___

01 Today I felt...

Draw your face here. Were you happy, laughing, nervous perhaps?

02 I felt happiest today when

_____

03 Gratitude
These are 2 things that really make me happy!

1 _____

2 _____

04 My happiness scale today

Where did you feel on the 'Happiness' scale today?

0 = Not very good   5= OK   10 = SENSATIONAL!

DATE: MON TUES WED THU FRI SAT SUN ___/___/___

01 I helped this person today..

Write below what you did to be kind.....

02 Gratitude. These are 3 things I am thankful for...

1 _____

2 _____

3 _____

03 I would rate today....

Color in your 'STAR' rating for today.

1 star = I didn't have a good day

5 stars = EXCELLENT!

MY UNICORN GRATITUDE JOURNAL

DATE: MON TUES WED THU FRI SAT SUN ___/___/___

01 Today I felt.....
Tick the face below...

02 Gratitude.
These are 3 things I am thankful for...

1 _____

2 _____

3 _____

03 Complete this sentence
What did you enjoy most about today?.......

Draw or Write Here

04 Today was:

MY UNICORN GRATITUDE JOURNAL

DATE: MON TUES WED THU FRI SAT SUN ___ / ___ / ___

01 My Happiness Rating

Circle how you feel?

- Happy
- Just OK
- I feel a little sad today

02 I would like to say thank you for...

1 _____
2 _____
3 _____

03 This person was kind today.

04 What did you enjoy most about today?.......

DATE: MON TUES WED THU FRI SAT SUN ___ / ___ / ___

01 Today I felt...

Draw your face here. Were you happy, laughing, nervous perhaps?

02 I felt happiest today when

_____

03 Gratitude
These are 2 things that really make me happy!

1 _____

2 _____

04 My happiness scale today

Where did you feel on the 'Happiness' scale today?

0 = Not very good   5 = OK   10 = SENSATIONAL!

MY UNICORN GRATITUDE JOURNAL

DATE: MON TUES WED THU FRI SAT SUN ___ / ___ / ___

01 I helped this person today..

Write below what you did to be kind.....

02 Gratitude. These are 3 things I am thankful for...

1 _____

2 _____

3 _____

03 I would rate today....
Color in your 'STAR' rating for today.
1 star = I didn't have a good day
5 stars = EXCELLENT!

DATE: MON TUES WED THU FRI SAT SUN _____ / _____ / _____

01 Today I felt.....
Tick the face below...

02 Gratitude.
These are 3 things I am thankful for...

1 _____

2 _____

3 _____

03 Complete this sentence
What did you enjoy most about today?....... Draw or Write Here

04 Today was:

MY UNICORN GRATITUDE JOURNAL

DATE: MON TUES WED THU FRI SAT SUN ___ / ___ / ___

01 My Happiness Rating

Circle how you feel?

Happy

Just OK

I feel a little sad today

02 I would like to say thank you for...

1 _____

2 _____

3 _____

03 This person was kind today.

04 What did you enjoy most about today?.......

DATE: MON TUES WED THU FRI SAT SUN ___ / ___ / ___

01 Today I felt...

Draw your face here. Were you happy, laughing, nervous perhaps?

02 I felt happiest today when

_____

03 Gratitude
These are 2 things that really make me happy!

1 _____

2 _____

04 My happiness scale today

Where did you feel on the 'Happiness' scale today?

0 = Not very good   5= OK   10 = SENSATIONAL!

MY UNICORN
GRATITUDE JOURNAL

DATE: MON TUES WED THU FRI SAT SUN ___ / ___ / ___

01 I helped this person today..

Write below what you did to be kind.....

02 Gratitude. These are 3 things I am thankful for...

1 _____

2 _____

3 _____

03 I would rate today....
Color in your 'STAR' rating for today.
1 star = I didn't have a good day
5 stars = EXCELLENT!

MY UNICORN GRATITUDE JOURNAL

DATE: MON TUES WED THU FRI SAT SUN ___ / ___ / ___

01 Today I felt.....
Tick the face below...

02 Gratitude.
These are 3 things I am thankful for...

1 _____

2 _____

3 _____

03 Complete this sentence
What did you enjoy most about today?.......

Draw or Write Here

04 Today was:

MY UNICORN GRATITUDE JOURNAL

DATE: MON TUES WED THU FRI SAT SUN ___ / ___ / ___

01 My Happiness Rating

Circle how you feel?

Happy

Just OK

I feel a little sad today

02 I would like to say thank you for...

1 _____

2 _____

3 _____

03 This person was kind today.

04 What did you enjoy most about today?.......

DATE: MON TUES WED THU FRI SAT SUN ___ / ___ / ___

01 Today I felt...

Draw your face here. Were you happy, laughing, nervous perhaps?

02 I felt happiest today when

_____

03 Gratitude

These are 2 things that really make me happy!

1 _____

2 _____

04 My happiness scale today

Where did you feel on the 'Happiness' scale today?

0 = Not very good   5 = OK   10 = SENSATIONAL!

DATE: MON TUES WED THU FRI SAT SUN _____ / _____ / _____

01 I helped this person today..

Write below what you did to be kind.....

02 Gratitude. These are 3 things I am thankful for...

1 _____

2 _____

3 _____

03 I would rate today....

Color in your 'STAR' rating for today.

I star = I didn't have a good day

5 stars = EXCELLENT!

MY UNICORN
GRATITUDE JOURNAL

DATE: MON TUES WED THU FRI SAT SUN ___/___/___

01 Today I felt.....
Tick the face below...

02 Gratitude.
These are 3 things I am thankful for...

1 _____

2 _____

3 _____

03 Complete this sentence
What did you enjoy most about today?.......   Draw or Write Here

04 Today was:

MY UNICORN
GRATITUDE JOURNAL

DATE: MON TUES WED THU FRI SAT SUN ___/___/___

01 My Happiness Rating

Circle how you feel?

Happy

Just OK

I feel a little
sad today

02 I would like to say thank you for...

1 _____

2 _____

3 _____

03 This person was kind today.

04 What did you enjoy most about today?.......

DATE: MON TUES WED THU FRI SAT SUN ___ / ___ / ___

01 Today I felt...

Draw your face here. Were you happy, laughing, nervous perhaps?

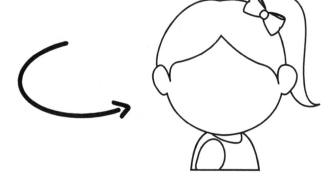

02 I felt happiest today when

_____

03 Gratitude
These are 2 things that really make me happy!

1 _____

2 _____

04 My happiness scale today

Where did you feel on the 'Happiness' scale today?

0 = Not very good   5 = OK   10 = SENSATIONAL!

MY UNICORN GRATITUDE JOURNAL

DATE: MON TUES WED THU FRI SAT SUN ___/___/___

01 I helped this person today..

Write below what you did to be kind.....

02 **Gratitude.** These are 3 things I am thankful for...

1 _____

2 _____

3 _____

03 **I would rate today....**
Color in your 'STAR' rating for today.
1 star = I didn't have a good day
5 stars = EXCELLENT!

MY UNICORN GRATITUDE JOURNAL

DATE: MON TUES WED THU FRI SAT SUN _____ / ____ / ____

01 Today I felt.....
Tick the face below...

02 Gratitude.
These are 3 things I am thankful for...

1 _____

2 _____

3 _____

03 Complete this sentence
What did you enjoy most about today?.......   Draw or Write Here

04 Today was:

MY UNICORN GRATITUDE JOURNAL

DATE: MON TUES WED THU FRI SAT SUN ___/___/___

01 My Happiness Rating

Circle how you feel?

Happy

Just OK

I feel a little sad today

02 I would like to say thank you for...

1 _____

2 _____

3 _____

03 This person was kind today.

04 What did you enjoy most about today?.......

DATE: MON TUES WED THU FRI SAT SUN ____ / ____ / ____

01 Today I felt...

Draw your face here. Were you happy, laughing, nervous perhaps?

02 I felt happiest today when

_____

03 Gratitude
These are 2 things that really make me happy!

1 _____

2 _____

04 My happiness scale today

Where did you feel on the 'Happiness' scale today?

0 = Not very good   5 = OK   10 = SENSATIONAL!

MY UNICORN GRATITUDE JOURNAL

DATE: MON TUES WED THU FRI SAT SUN ___/___/___

01 I helped this person today..

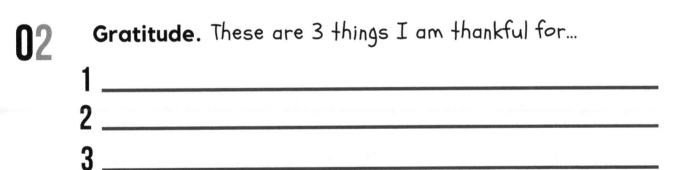

Write below what you did to be kind.....

02 Gratitude. These are 3 things I am thankful for...

1 _____

2 _____

3 _____

03 I would rate today....
Color in your 'STAR' rating for today.
1 star = I didn't have a good day
5 stars = EXCELLENT!

MY UNICORN
GRATITUDE JOURNAL

Congratulations! You are up to day 30.

It's time for you to look back over your gratitude journal and answer the following questions.

01 Moments

What were your favorite 3 things you did over the past 30 days?

1.
_____

2.
_____

3.
_____

02 Be Creative!

Draw a picture or stick a photo here that was a special moment for you over the past 30 days.

Color in the Unicorn and relax.

MY UNICORN GRATITUDE JOURNAL

Draw a picture or include a

favorite photo

MY UNICORN GRATITUDE JOURNAL

DATE: MON TUES WED THU FRI SAT SUN ___/___/___

01 I helped this person today..

Write below what you did to be kind.....

02 Gratitude. These are 3 things I am thankful for...

1 _____

2 _____

3 _____

03 I would rate today....
Color in your 'STAR' rating for today.
I star = I didn't have a good day
S stars = EXCELLENT!

DATE: MON TUES WED THU FRI SAT SUN ___ / ___ / ___

01 Today I felt.....
Tick the face below...

02 Gratitude.
These are 3 things I am thankful for...

1 _____

2 _____

3 _____

03 Complete this sentence
What did you enjoy most about today?.......

Draw or Write Here

04 Today was:

DATE: MON TUES WED THU FRI SAT SUN ____ / ____ / ____

01 My Happiness Rating

Circle how you feel?

Happy

Just OK

I feel a little sad today

02 I would like to say thank you for...

1 _____

2 _____

3 _____

03 This person was kind today.

04 What did you enjoy most about today?.......

MY UNICORN GRATITUDE JOURNAL

DATE: MON TUES WED THU FRI SAT SUN ___ / ___ / ___

01 Today I felt...

Draw your face here. Were you happy, laughing, nervous perhaps?

02 I felt happiest today when

_____

03 Gratitude
These are 2 things that really make me happy!

1 _____

2 _____

04 My happiness scale today

Where did you feel on the 'Happiness' scale today?

0 = Not very good   5 = OK   10 = SENSATIONAL!

DATE: MON TUES WED THU FRI SAT SUN _____ / _____ / _____

01 I helped this person today..

♡ ♡ ♥ ♡ ♡

Write below what you did to be kind.....

{ }

02 Gratitude. These are 3 things I am thankful for...

1 _____

2 _____

3 _____

03 I would rate today....
Color in your 'STAR' rating for today.
I star = I didn't have a good day
S stars = EXCELLENT!

DATE: MON TUES WED THU FRI SAT SUN ___ / ___ / ___

01 Today I felt.....
Tick the face below...

02 Gratitude.
These are 3 things I am thankful for...

1 _____

2 _____

3 _____

03 Complete this sentence
What did you enjoy most about today?.......

Draw or Write Here

04 Today was:

MY UNICORN GRATITUDE JOURNAL

DATE: MON TUES WED THU FRI SAT SUN ___/___/___

01 My Happiness Rating
Circle how you feel?

- Happy
- Just OK
- I feel a little sad today

02 I would like to say thank you for...
1 _____
2 _____
3 _____

03 This person was kind today.

04 What did you enjoy most about today?.......

DATE: MON TUES WED THU FRI SAT SUN ___ / ___ / ___

01 Today I felt...

Draw your face here. Were you happy, laughing, nervous perhaps?

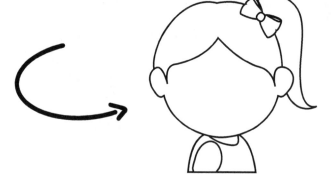

02 I felt happiest today when

_____

03 Gratitude
These are 2 things that really make me happy!

1 _____

2 _____

04 My happiness scale today

Where did you feel on the 'Happiness' scale today?

0 = Not very good   5 = OK   10 = SENSATIONAL!

DATE: MON TUES WED THU FRI SAT SUN ___/___/___

01 I helped this person today..

Write below what you did to be kind.....

{ }

02 Gratitude. These are 3 things I am thankful for...

1 _____

2 _____

3 _____

03 I would rate today....

Color in your 'STAR' rating for today.
1 star = I didn't have a good day
5 stars = EXCELLENT!

MY UNICORN GRATITUDE JOURNAL

DATE: MON TUES WED THU FRI SAT SUN ___/___/___

01 Today I felt.....
Tick the face below...

02 Gratitude.
These are 3 things I am thankful for...

1 _____

2 _____

3 _____

03 Complete this sentence
What did you enjoy most about today?.......

Draw or write Here

04 Today was:

MY UNICORN GRATITUDE JOURNAL

DATE: MON TUES WED THU FRI SAT SUN ___ / ___ / ___

01 My Happiness Rating

Circle how you feel?

Happy

Just OK

I feel a little sad today

02 I would like to say thank you for...

1 _____

2 _____

3 _____

03 This person was kind today.

04 What did you enjoy most about today?.......

DATE: MON TUES WED THU FRI SAT SUN ____ / ____ / ____

01 Today I felt...

Draw your face here. Were you happy, laughing, nervous perhaps?

02 I felt happiest today when

_____

03 Gratitude
These are 2 things that really make me happy!

1 _____

2 _____

04 My happiness scale today

Where did you feel on the 'Happiness' scale today?

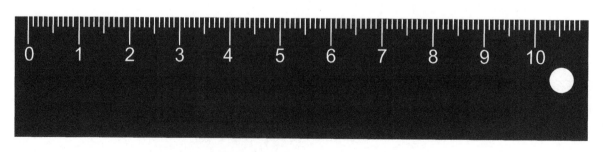

0 = Not very good   5 = OK   10 = SENSATIONAL!

DATE: MON TUES WED THU FRI SAT SUN   __/__/__

01 I helped this person today..

Write below what you did to be kind.....

02 Gratitude. These are 3 things I am thankful for...

1 _____
2 _____
3 _____

03 I would rate today....
Color in your 'STAR' rating for today.
I star = I didn't have a good day
S stars = EXCELLENT!

DATE: MON TUES WED THU FRI SAT SUN ___ / ___ / ___

01 Today I felt.....
Tick the face below...

02 Gratitude.
These are 3 things I am thankful for...

1 _____

2 _____

3 _____

03 Complete this sentence
What did you enjoy most about today?.......

Draw or Write Here

04 Today was:

DATE: MON TUES WED THU FRI SAT SUN _____ / _____ / _____

01 My Happiness Rating

Circle how you feel?

Happy

Just OK

I feel a little sad today

02 I would like to say thank you for...

1 _____

2 _____

3 _____

03 This person was kind today.

04 What did you enjoy most about today?.......

DATE: MON TUES WED THU FRI SAT SUN ___ / ___ / ___

01 Today I felt...

Draw your face here. Were you happy, laughing, nervous perhaps?

02 I felt happiest today when

_____

03 Gratitude
These are 2 things that really make me happy!

1 _____

2 _____

04 My happiness scale today

Where did you feel on the 'Happiness' scale today?

0 = Not very good   5 = OK   10 = SENSATIONAL!

MY UNICORN GRATITUDE JOURNAL

DATE: MON TUES WED THU FRI SAT SUN ___/___/___

01 I helped this person today..

♡ ♡ ♡ ♡ ♡

Write below what you did to be kind.....

{ }

02 Gratitude. These are 3 things I am thankful for...

1 _____

2 _____

3 _____

03 I would rate today....
Color in your 'STAR' rating for today.
1 star = I didn't have a good day
5 stars = EXCELLENT!

DATE: MON TUES WED THU FRI SAT SUN ___/___/___

01 Today I felt.....
Tick the face below...

02 Gratitude.
These are 3 things I am thankful for...

1 _____

2 _____

3 _____

03 Complete this sentence
What did you enjoy most about today?.......

Draw or Write Here

04 Today was:

MY UNICORN GRATITUDE JOURNAL

DATE: MON TUES WED THU FRI SAT SUN ___/___/___

01 My Happiness Rating

Circle how you feel?

Happy

Just OK

I feel a little sad today

02 I would like to say thank you for...

1 _____

2 _____

3 _____

03 This person was kind today.

04 What did you enjoy most about today?.......

DATE: MON TUES WED THU FRI SAT SUN ___ / ___ / ___

01 Today I felt...

Draw your face here. Were you happy, laughing, nervous perhaps?

02 I felt happiest today when

_____

03 Gratitude
These are 2 things that really make me happy!

1 _____

2 _____

04 My happiness scale today

Where did you feel on the 'Happiness' scale today?

0 = Not very good   5= OK   10 = SENSATIONAL!

MY UNICORN GRATITUDE JOURNAL

DATE: MON TUES WED THU FRI SAT SUN   __ / __ / __

01   I helped this person today..

Write below what you did to be kind.....

02   Gratitude. These are 3 things I am thankful for...

1 _____

2 _____

3 _____

03   I would rate today....

Color in your 'STAR' rating for today.

I star = I didn't have a good day

5 stars = EXCELLENT!

MY UNICORN GRATITUDE JOURNAL

DATE: MON TUES WED THU FRI SAT SUN ___ / ___ / ___

01 Today I felt.....
Tick the face below...

😊 😎 😟 😢 😠 😉

02 Gratitude.
These are 3 things I am thankful for...

1 _____

2 _____

3 _____

03 Complete this sentence
What did you enjoy most about today?.......

Draw or Write Here

04 Today was:

MY UNICORN GRATITUDE JOURNAL

DAY

53

DATE: MON TUES WED THU FRI SAT SUN ___/___/___

01 My Happiness Rating

Circle how you feel?

- Happy
- Just OK
- I feel a little sad today

02 I would like to say thank you for...

1 _____

2 _____

3 _____

03 This person was kind today.

04 What did you enjoy most about today?.......

DATE: MON TUES WED THU FRI SAT SUN ___ / ___ / ___

01 Today I felt...

Draw your face here. Were you happy, laughing, nervous perhaps?

02 I felt happiest today when

_____

03 Gratitude
These are 2 things that really make me happy!

1 _____

2 _____

04 My happiness scale today

Where did you feel on the 'Happiness' scale today?

0 = Not very good   5= OK   10 = SENSATIONAL!

MY UNICORN GRATITUDE JOURNAL

DATE: MON TUES WED THU FRI SAT SUN _____ / ___ / ___

01 I helped this person today..

Write below what you did to be kind.....

02 Gratitude. These are 3 things I am thankful for...

1 _____

2 _____

3 _____

03 I would rate today....
Color in your 'STAR' rating for today.
1 star = I didn't have a good day
5 stars = EXCELLENT!

MY UNICORN
GRATITUDE JOURNAL

DATE: MON TUES WED THU FRI SAT SUN _____ / _____ / _____

01 Today I felt.....
Tick the face below...

02 Gratitude.
These are 3 things I am thankful for...

1 _____

2 _____

3 _____

03 Complete this sentence
What did you enjoy most about today?.......

Draw or Write Here

04 Today was:

DATE: MON TUES WED THU FRI SAT SUN ___/___/___

01 My Happiness Rating

Circle how you feel?

Happy

Just OK

I feel a little sad today

02 I would like to say thank you for...

1 _____

2 _____

3 _____

03 This person was kind today.

04 What did you enjoy most about today?.......

DATE: MON TUES WED THU FRI SAT SUN ___ / ___ / ___

01 Today I felt...

Draw your face here. Were you happy, laughing, nervous perhaps?

02 I felt happiest today when

_____

03 Gratitude
These are 2 things that really make me happy!

1 _____

2 _____

04 My happiness scale today

Where did you feel on the 'Happiness' scale today?

0 = Not very good   5 = OK   10 = SENSATIONAL!

MY UNICORN GRATITUDE JOURNAL

DATE: MON TUES WED THU FRI SAT SUN ___/___/___

01 I helped this person today..

Write below what you did to be kind.....

02 Gratitude. These are 3 things I am thankful for...

1 _____

2 _____

3 _____

03 I would rate today....

Color in your 'STAR' rating for today.

1 star = I didn't have a good day

5 stars = EXCELLENT!

Congratulations! You are up to day 60.

It's time for you to look back over your gratitude journal and answer the following questions.

01 Moments

What were your favorite 3 things you did over the past 30 days?

1. _____

2. _____

3. _____

02 Be Creative!

Draw a picture or stick a photo here that was a special moment for you over the past 30 days.

Relax and color in your unicorn

DATE: MON TUES WED THU FRI SAT SUN ___ / ___ / ___

01 I helped this person today..

Write below what you did to be kind.....

02 Gratitude. These are 3 things I am thankful for...

1 _____

2 _____

3 _____

03 I would rate today....

Color in your 'STAR' rating for today.

I star = I didn't have a good day

S stars = EXCELLENT!

MY UNICORN GRATITUDE JOURNAL

DATE: MON TUES WED THU FRI SAT SUN ___/___/___

01 Today I felt.....
Tick the face below...

02 Gratitude.
These are 3 things I am thankful for...

1 _____

2 _____

3 _____

03 Complete this sentence
What did you enjoy most about today?.......

Draw or Write Here

04 Today was:

DATE: MON TUES WED THU FRI SAT SUN ___ / ___ / ___

01 My Happiness Rating

Circle how you feel?

Happy

Just OK

I feel a little sad today

02 I would like to say thank you for...

1 _____

2 _____

3 _____

03 This person was kind today.

04 What did you enjoy most about today?.......

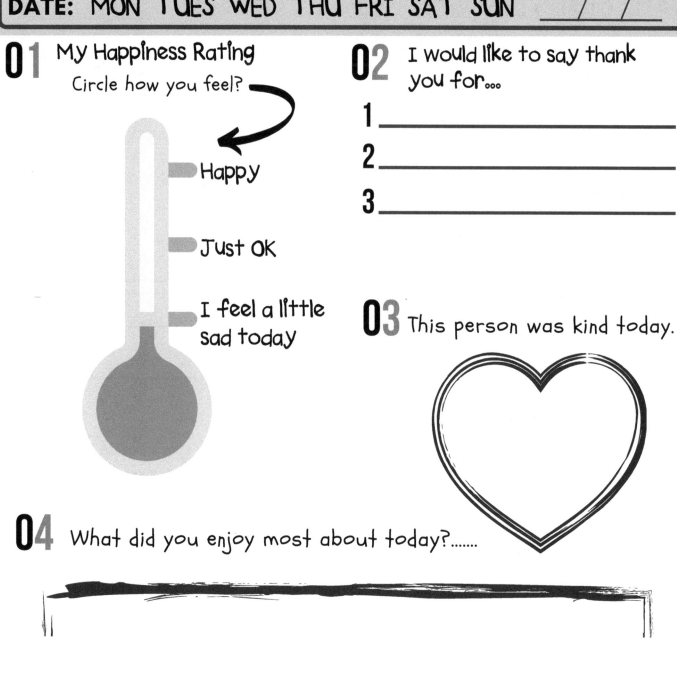

DATE: MON TUES WED THU FRI SAT SUN ___ / ___ / ___

01 Today I felt...

Draw your face here. Were you happy, laughing, nervous perhaps?

02 I felt happiest today when

_____

03 Gratitude
These are 2 things that really make me happy!

1 _____

2 _____

04 My happiness scale today

Where did you feel on the 'Happiness' scale today?

0 = Not very good   5 = OK   10 = SENSATIONAL!

MY UNICORN GRATITUDE JOURNAL

DATE: MON TUES WED THU FRI SAT SUN ___/___/___

01 I helped this person today..

Write below what you did to be kind.....

02 Gratitude. These are 3 things I am thankful for...

1 _____

2 _____

3 _____

03 I would rate today....

Color in your 'STAR' rating for today.

I star = I didn't have a good day

5 stars = EXCELLENT!

MY UNICORN
GRATITUDE JOURNAL

DATE: MON TUES WED THU FRI SAT SUN _____ / ____ / ____

01 Today I felt.....
Tick the face below...

02 Gratitude.
These are 3 things I am thankful for...

1 _____

2 _____

3 _____

03 Complete this sentence
What did you enjoy most about today?....... Draw or write Here

04 Today was:

MY UNICORN GRATITUDE JOURNAL

DATE: MON TUES WED THU FRI SAT SUN ___ / ___ / ___

01 My Happiness Rating

Circle how you feel?

- Happy
- Just OK
- I feel a little sad today

02 I would like to say thank you for...

1 _____

2 _____

3 _____

03 This person was kind today.

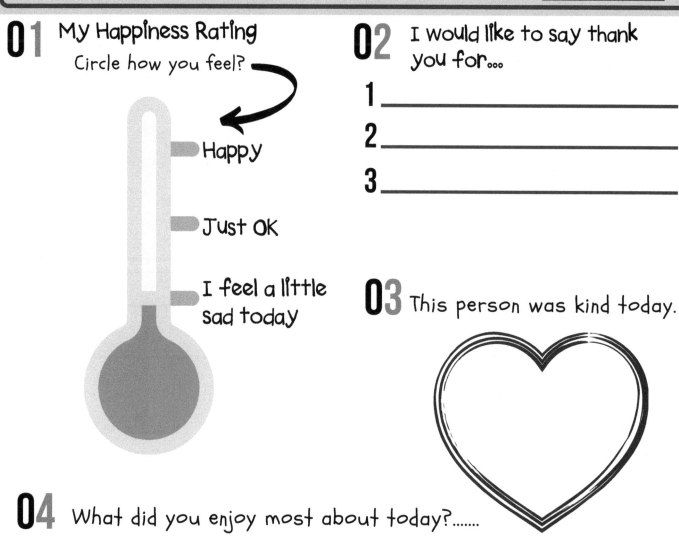

04 What did you enjoy most about today?.......

MY UNICORN
GRATITUDE JOURNAL

DATE: MON TUES WED THU FRI SAT SUN ___/___/___

01 Today I felt...

Draw your face here. Were you happy, laughing, nervous perhaps?

02 I felt happiest today when

_____

03 Gratitude
These are 2 things that really make me happy!

1 _____

2 _____

04 My happiness scale today

Where did you feel on the 'Happiness' scale today?

0 = Not very good   5= OK   10 = SENSATIONAL!

DATE: MON TUES WED THU FRI SAT SUN ___/___/___

01 I helped this person today..

Write below what you did to be kind.....

02 Gratitude. These are 3 things I am thankful for...

1 _____

2 _____

3 _____

03 I would rate today....
Color in your 'STAR' rating for today.
I star = I didn't have a good day
5 stars = EXCELLENT!

MY UNICORN
GRATITUDE JOURNAL

DATE: MON TUES WED THU FRI SAT SUN ___/___/___

01 Today I felt.....
Tick the face below...

😊 😎 😟 😢 😠 😉

02 Gratitude.
These are 3 things I am thankful for...

1 _____

2 _____

3 _____

03 Complete this sentence
What did you enjoy most about today?....... Draw or Write Here

04 Today was:

MY UNICORN GRATITUDE JOURNAL

DATE: MON TUES WED THU FRI SAT SUN ___ / ___ / ___

01 My Happiness Rating

Circle how you feel?

Happy

Just OK

I feel a little sad today

02 I would like to say thank you for...

1 _____

2 _____

3 _____

03 This person was kind today.

04 What did you enjoy most about today?.......

DATE: MON TUES WED THU FRI SAT SUN ___ / ___ / ___

01 Today I felt...

Draw your face here. Were you happy, laughing, nervous perhaps?

02 I felt happiest today when

_____

03 Gratitude
These are 2 things that really make me happy!

1 _____

2 _____

04 My happiness scale today

Where did you feel on the 'Happiness' scale today?

0 = Not very good   5 = OK   10 = SENSATIONAL!

MY UNICORN GRATITUDE JOURNAL

DATE: MON TUES WED THU FRI SAT SUN ___/___/___

01 I helped this person today..

Write below what you did to be kind.....

02 Gratitude. These are 3 things I am thankful for...

1 _____
2 _____
3 _____

03 I would rate today....
Color in your 'STAR' rating for today.
1 star = I didn't have a good day
S stars = EXCELLENT!

MY UNICORN GRATITUDE JOURNAL

DAY

74

DATE: MON TUES WED THU FRI SAT SUN ___ / ___ / ___

01 Today I felt.....
Tick the face below...

02 Gratitude.
These are 3 things I am thankful for...

1 _____

2 _____

3 _____

03 Complete this sentence
What did you enjoy most about today?....... Draw or Write Here

04 Today was:

DATE: MON TUES WED THU FRI SAT SUN ___ / ___ / ___

01 My Happiness Rating

Circle how you feel?

Happy

Just OK

I feel a little sad today

02 I would like to say thank you for...

1 _____

2 _____

3 _____

03 This person was kind today.

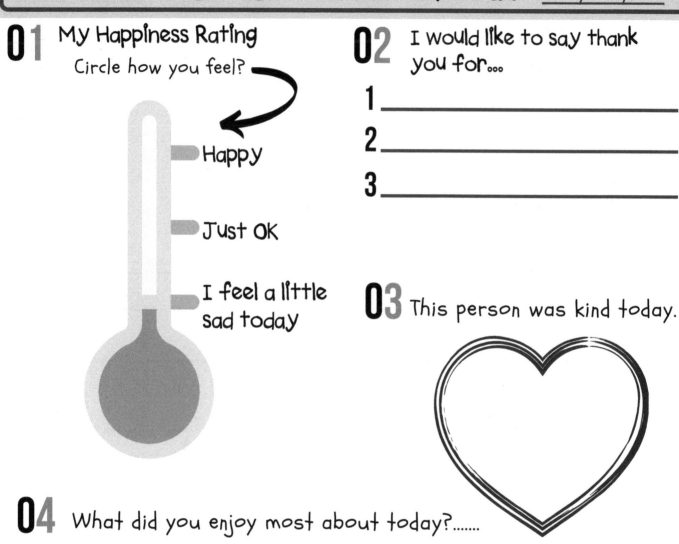

04 What did you enjoy most about today?.......

MY UNICORN GRATITUDE JOURNAL

DAY

76

DATE: MON TUES WED THU FRI SAT SUN ____ / ____ / ____

01 Today I felt...

Draw your face here. Were you happy, laughing, nervous perhaps?

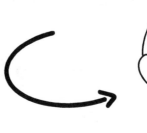

02 I felt happiest today when

_____

03 Gratitude
These are 2 things that really make me happy!

1 _____

2 _____

04 My happiness scale today

Where did you feel on the 'Happiness' scale today?

0 = Not very good   5 = OK   10 = SENSATIONAL!

MY UNICORN
GRATITUDE JOURNAL

DATE: MON TUES WED THU FRI SAT SUN ___ / ___ / ___

01 **I helped this person today..**

Write below what you did to be kind.....

02 **Gratitude.** These are 3 things I am thankful for...

1 _____

2 _____

3 _____

03 **I would rate today....**
Color in your 'STAR' rating for today.
1 star = I didn't have a good day
5 stars = EXCELLENT!

DATE: MON TUES WED THU FRI SAT SUN ___/___/___

01 Today I felt.....
Tick the face below...

02 Gratitude.
These are 3 things I am thankful for...

1 _____

2 _____

3 _____

03 Complete this sentence
What did you enjoy most about today?....... Draw or Write Here

04 Today was:

MY UNICORN GRATITUDE JOURNAL

DATE: MON TUES WED THU FRI SAT SUN ___ / ___ / ___

01 My Happiness Rating

Circle how you feel?

- Happy
- Just OK
- I feel a little sad today

02 I would like to say thank you for...

1 _____

2 _____

3 _____

03 This person was kind today.

04 What did you enjoy most about today?.......

DATE: MON TUES WED THU FRI SAT SUN ____/____/____

01 Today I felt...

Draw your face here. Were you happy, laughing, nervous perhaps?

02 I felt happiest today when

_____

03 Gratitude
These are 2 things that really make me happy!

1 _____

2 _____

04 My happiness scale today

Where did you feel on the 'Happiness' scale today?

0 = Not very good   5= OK   10 = SENSATIONAL!

DATE: MON TUES WED THU FRI SAT SUN ___ / ___ / ___

01 I helped this person today..

Write below what you did to be kind.....

02 Gratitude. These are 3 things I am thankful for...

1 _____

2 _____

3 _____

03 I would rate today....
Color in your 'STAR' rating for today.
I star = I didn't have a good day
S stars = EXCELLENT!

DATE: MON TUES WED THU FRI SAT SUN ___/___/___

01 Today I felt.....
Tick the face below...

02 Gratitude.
These are 3 things I am thankful for...

1 _____

2 _____

3 _____

03 Complete this sentence
What did you enjoy most about today?....... Draw or Write Here

04 Today was:

DATE: MON TUES WED THU FRI SAT SUN ___/___/___

01 My Happiness Rating

Circle how you feel?

Happy

Just OK

I feel a little sad today

02 I would like to say thank you for...

1 _____

2 _____

3 _____

03 This person was kind today.

04 What did you enjoy most about today?.......

DATE: MON TUES WED THU FRI SAT SUN ___ / ___ / ___

01 Today I felt...

Draw your face here. Were you happy, laughing, nervous perhaps?

02 I felt happiest today when

_____

03 Gratitude
These are 2 things that really make me happy!

1 _____

2 _____

04 My happiness scale today

Where did you feel on the 'Happiness' scale today?

0 = Not very good   5= OK   10 = SENSATIONAL!

DATE: MON TUES WED THU FRI SAT SUN ___/___/___

01 I helped this person today..

Write below what you did to be kind.....

02 Gratitude. These are 3 things I am thankful for...

1 _____

2 _____

3 _____

03 I would rate today....
Color in your 'STAR' rating for today.
1 star = I didn't have a good day
5 stars = EXCELLENT!

MY UNICORN
GRATITUDE JOURNAL

DATE: MON TUES WED THU FRI SAT SUN __/__/__

01 I helped this person today..

Write below what you did to be kind.....

02 Gratitude. These are 3 things I am thankful for...

1 _____

2 _____

3 _____

03 I would rate today....
Color in your 'STAR' rating for today.
I star = I didn't have a good day
5 stars = EXCELLENT!

DATE: MON TUES WED THU FRI SAT SUN ___ / ___ / ___

01 Today I felt.....
Tick the face below...

02 Gratitude.
These are 3 things I am thankful for...

1 _____

2 _____

3 _____

03 Complete this sentence
What did you enjoy most about today?....... Draw or Write Here

04 Today was:

DATE: MON TUES WED THU FRI SAT SUN _____ / ___ / ___

01 My Happiness Rating

Circle how you feel?

Happy

Just OK

I feel a little sad today

02 I would like to say thank you for...

1 _____

2 _____

3 _____

03 This person was kind today.

04 What did you enjoy most about today?.......

DATE: MON TUES WED THU FRI SAT SUN ___/___/___

01 Today I felt...

Draw your face here. Were you happy, laughing, nervous perhaps?

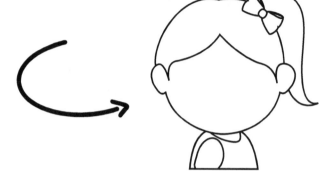

02 I felt happiest today when

_____

03 Gratitude
These are 2 things that really make me happy!

1 _____

2 _____

04 My happiness scale today

Where did you feel on the 'Happiness' scale today?

0 = Not very good   5= OK   10 = SENSATIONAL!

MY UNICORN GRATITUDE JOURNAL

AMAZING! You have completed your 90 day journal. CONGRATULATIONS!!

It's time for you to look back over your gratitude journal and answer the following questions.

01 Moments

What were your favorite 3 things you did over the past 90 days?

1. _____

2. _____

3. _____

02 Be Creative!

Draw a picture or stick a photo here that was a special moment for you since starting your gratitude journal?

MY UNICORN GRATITUDE JOURNAL

90 Day Journal Notes

Write here whatever you feel like. Is there something special you would like to include in your journal?

_____

_____

_____

_____

_____

_____

_____

_____

_____

"Nothing new can come into your life unless you are grateful for what you already have"

- Michael Bernard

About the Author

Romney Nelson is a #1 Amazon Best Selling Author and Leading Australian Goal Setting and Habit Development Expert. He commenced his career as a primary and secondary school teacher working in some of the most well-known schools in Australia, including Head of Faculty positions in Oxford and Wimbledon, United Kingdom.

Romney authored his first resource, PE on the GO; a physical education resource for teachers in 2009 and in 2019 in founded The Life Graduate Publishing Group and created The Daily Goal Tracker, a powerful and practical resource developed to Create, Track and Achieve your goals. In 2020, Romney became an Amazon Best Selling Author with the release of The Habit Switch. His other books include Magnetic Goals, The Daily Goal Tracker, The 5 Minute Morning Journal and various educational and children's books.

www.thelifegraduate.com/bookstore

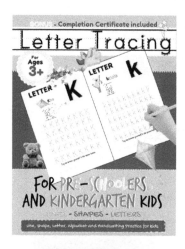

CPSIA information can be obtained
at www.ICGtesting.com
Printed in the USA
BVHW051532231221
624755BV00005B/206

9 781922 568786